John Vance Cheney, William Doxey

Ninette. A Redwoods Idyll

John Vance Cheney, William Doxey

Ninette. A Redwoods Idyll

ISBN/EAN: 9783743305281

Manufactured in Europe, USA, Canada, Australia, Japa

Cover: Foto ©ninafisch / pixelio.de

Manufactured and distributed by brebook publishing software
(www.brebook.com)

John Vance Cheney, William Doxey

Ninette. A Redwoods Idyll

WAS in the days when through the Golden Gate
The good ships bore the builders of a State.
Why was it royal Adolph could not be
Hail-fellow in this lordly company,
Lordly as ever from the ends of earth
Was drawn and marshalled for a city's birth!
The palaces of chance with clinking stream
Of silver, ringing showers of gold,—the dream
Of Danaë come true, they were for him,
And yet the fine gold, how was it waxed dim!
By day and night the gilded ways he strode,
Stalwart as any; out the Mission Road
Dashed side by side with maddest cavalier
That jingled spur; but ever in his ear
Sounded the counsel of the white-haired sire,
Whom he had rescued from the hamlet fire.

Glorious old roamer! many years before
Famed Forty-Nine he knew the Golden Shore;
And well a youth might heed the thing he said.
Bending benignantly his noble head
As bend the oaks of Napa when they lean
To meet the wild oat in its April green.
"In olden woods the rarest mosses be,
Old heads are white with treasure. Come to me."
These were the words, too round to be denied;
And then was there not something said beside,
About the "bird" Ninette, "her mother's child,
Orphaned down in the burning southern wild"!
These last were chance words, dropped in by the way,
But to a young heart — let the young hearts say.
"In olden woods"— it echoed on and on;
The boat slipped from her mooring, the boy was gone.
Slow out of sight Yerba Buena passed,
Next rusty Alcatraz, and Angel last;
Behind, now, lay the windy town, the bay
Rippling and glistening in the perfect day;
Before, the valley of the oat and oak.

Ere long lulled off to slumber, when he woke
'T was time to quit the boat, and with a will
To thrid the oaks far as the western hill,
    Where the guide, Cactus, waited in the shade.
The wind was stirring, and the bur-oaks laid
Great shadows, black along the blanching grass,
Matted so thick it would not let him pass
Where it was rankest; clear, between the swells
Of wind, clear, merry, rang the blackbird bells,
While gurgling music, hurrying note to note.
Spilled from the starling's overflowing throat.
And it was twilight ere he reached the guide
Lounging upon the scenty mountain-side,
Young, dusky Cactus, lithe and debonair
A slave as ever fawned on lady fair;
And deep the sun was sunk into the west
The hour they reached the Redwoods and the " Nest."

'T WAS dawn; at the first calling of the quail
Adolph appeared. Below, the oaken vale
And plunging spines of interjacent hills
Were all in fog, the dense white fog that fills
The world up, there, till broad-backed ranges be
Mere porpoises swimming a vapor sea.
High over the white sea the sire had set
His hearty morning meal. No others yet
Were stirring, and the two, as hill-gods might,
Sat there, and ate, then storied till the light
Was in full glory; when strode they forth, again
And yet again to scan their great domain.
'Helena's cap is off; now is the hour;
Behold it, boy,— old Mother Nature's power!"
It was the sire, not half his welcome said,
Hymning his Redwoods heaven as on he led.
'Here has she set on high, and there laid low,
As pleased her. Guttruff from yon rock can throw
The sight across seven ranges; turn that way,
And he can count the white sails on the bay.
How now? And there be wonders in the West?
We hear the stars here, we in Eagle Nest."

The squirrels flowing
    round them, the pert jay
Mocking the hawks, the highholes at their play,
The golden-robin with his vigorous tune
Singing his heart into the heart of June;
The lusty quail lifting amid it all
The happiest mountain sound, wild love's own call.—
Attended thus, moved slowly sire and guest
Till come upon the "one bird" of the Nest.
'T was in one of those fringy, winding places
Where close the clover-velvet interlaces,
And the dwarf oak and little evergreen,
Lovers, in one another's arms are seen.
Under a manzanita, glossy, dark,
Her yellow head, leaned on its winy bark,
Made sunlight there. "Sire," Adolph sighed, "all Greece
Might well have sailed to fetch that golden fleece."
Nor was the sighing fainter since the child
Was woman rather, blossoming in the wild,
With song and laughter. It was lesson-time,
And, taught of brooks, she rippled rhyme to rhyme:—

"Catch-fly, clocks, and columbine,
   Whose am I if he is mine?

"Blue-curls, bindweed, baby-eyes,
   Love is cruel when he tries.

"Hound's-tongue, nightshade, meadow-rue,
   I'll have lover none but you.

"Pin-bloom, pipe-vine, pimpernel,
   This, sweet naughty, you know well

"Shepherd's-purse and shooting-star,
   Strangest folk all lovers are.

"Silverweed and thimbleberry,
   Ho, my heart, but we are merry!

"Bleeding-heart and virgin's-bower,
   Now it is the lover's hour.

"Stonecrop, stickseed, tiger-lily,
   He will love me—will he, will he?

"Knot-grass and forget-me-not,
   Let him swear it on the spot."

"THE larkspur, painted-brush and poppy flame,
Ay, every peeping sweet without a name,
All, in those sunsets under foot; the hues
Of purple and of scarlet, greens and blues,
How have those beauties all their beauty blown
Into one blossom, all the flow'ret's own
That woke, one morn, and was a human face!"
Adolph leaned forward, poised as for the chase.
And carolling Ninette? The list'ning wood
Breathed out a shape to her. So bright he stood
She could not tell whether he was of earth
Or owed the old divinities his birth,
Sent down to be her father's friend, since he
So honored them. Her blood ran riot, she
Could feel the traitor shame-spots creep and grow;
The ruddy god—would he not see, not know
    Each silly thought, and tell it, too, and set
    All heaven a-laughing? Innocent Ninette,
    A silly child indeed to bleed with shame
Before a god that could not speak her name,
So dumb he was; one to be led away
That he might arm to woo another day.

Age yet may serve young love. High on the rock
Whence shines the bay, our lover could unlock
His tongue; unsparing spent he on and on
Until it seemed all love's best words were gone.
The good sire heard, but as one hears in dream;
His mind was back there by the bay. The gleam,
The growing wind, the smoke, the jam of drays,
The furious hurry in the narrow ways;
At last the wall, the fragile, hanging wall,
And then the cheering—and the blank. Life, all,
Again 't was saved him by the peerless boy,
And in a torrent broke his father's joy:—
"Once more, once more, kind gods, I find a man
To lift the heart up. Stand, Greek Puritan,
That I may look, gaze till my sight, long dull,
Whets it upon you, strong and beautiful.
Methinks those were your fellows, brown-haired boy,
Who brewed the storm before the walls of Troy;
There had you buckled armor with the best,
Shining to stir the hovering goddess' breast.

I said, to-morrow you should go to dig,
To gorge you in the tawny hills; but, big
With fondness, I so tyrannous am grown
I will to keep you. Leave me not alone
Till th' autumn rains. The gold will
    wait. Boy, know
Here in the wild I wandered years ago,
And can, asleep, discourse of rock and sand
To plague your wisest. Put in mine your hand:
You shall have gold in heaps, then, surfeited,
(If she will yield it) her own golden head.
For two years, boy, she bides my one bird still,
And then, why, then as she and Heaven will."

THE summer went; and overhead the gray
Was growing on the blue. If graver lay
Ninette sang now, the measure ran too free
For true-love bonds, for captive minstrelsy :—

"Run away, love, and leave to me
   The way of the bird and the way of the bee:
      Flower to flower down to the mead,
   Mead to mead over the vale,
      Vale to vale as the sunbeams lead,
   On to the sea and the endless sail.

      "No, no, love, I will not stop,
         The butterfly swings in the thistle-top;
            Rock, rock, in the sunny weather,
         Song of the bird and sweet of the bee,
            Just the day and I together,—
         That's the life and the love for me.

   "Fie, fie, love, bliss enough for me
      The song of the bird, the sweet of the bee:
         Flower to flower down from the hill,
      Flower to flower down to the dale,
         Field to field as the free winds will,
      Ho, for the sea and the endless sail!"

"Nay, Nature; flowers will waken at
      her feet,
          Untimely, wrongly flourish in the sweet
Of her false Spring. Ay, quickened, they will blow;
Like her, will wake and waste, and never know."
So grieved the boy the while he secret heard
The burden of the merry Redwoods bird.
Lorn Adolph! Song that can deceive the year
May be too subtle for a lover's ear;
Chance, other measures sang the merry bird
Deep in her heart.

And now the sky was blurred,
And over hill and valley woven and spread
Dull, slumbrous color for the season dead.
The sire could not sit calmly at his door
And let the boy go, but, well on before,
His voice startling the rabbit and the quail,
Must see him to the forking of the trail:
"Straight as the pigeon points will run the way,
With Cactus for your guide. He must not stay;
It is no Sabbath journey, and we need
The shoot of darkness here. The nightshade-seed
Is brother's dog, his crutch; and past a doubt —
The voice dropped now—the girl were lost without
Her Shadow. Lad, the goddess—does she chide
Or sway the battle to my hero's side?
How reads the omen?"

                    "I have kept my vow,
Good sire; so, pray you, let me answer now."

A TWELVE-MONTH passed ere fortune brought
    the sire
Fresh fuel for his pioneeric fire:—
"Right royal robbery, boy! but more, more yet.
By Napa's oak and by the bird Ninette,
Play on, throw on; it shall be kingdoms. More,
More yet, more, more. Away! But not before
Some word be left may please a lass's ear.
You scarce have seen Ninette; too sharp, I fear,
The thorns of honor." Slowly Adolph said,
His brow bared, "Not the lightest little thread
That flies, far shining, from that golden head,
Or wanders down that wondrous neck, love-led,
Has felt a breath from me."

Another June,
And Adolph came to hear the fairy tune
Of air and laughter, even the same he heard
It seemed an age before. The wilding bird
Sang on the same old elfin-measured song,
Trilling along the hills; the warm day long
The same far ditty, while with lighter feet
The little breezes danced to it, and sweet
The mating birds, 'mong the madroño boughs,
Wove snatches of it in their lover's vows.
Two years had wrought a change. But few days more
Were left the uncle; haggard, now, as hoar
Was he that came to hide him from his kind,
The scholar, hurt in body and in mind,
Ninette's tutor, from whom no plant that grows
Could keep the secret of its leaves and blows.
Time had been busy: Gorgon, grim old dog,
Followed her master's heel with feebler jog,
While Hector, the pet elk, had sprouted horn
Fit for the front of vanished Unicorn.
And not the same was Cactus; like his charge
And playmate, Hector, he had sprung to large
And dangerous size. To some old tameless race
He pointed, with his native leopard's grace
And withy sinew.

3

And Ninette, the bird,
The one bird of the Nest—love had no word
To name her change. "Good sire," the lover said,
"The child, as any eye may see, has fled,
And I must woo a woman."
                              "Jacob, boy,
Winced not at plump seven year. The gods help Troy,
And great Achilles sulks."

                    "Easy the gold
Was rifled from the sands. There was I bold
To lead; could swing a thief up, hear his groan,
Unmoved; for play could break a bully's bone,
And laugh, and bid him mend it. Now, I whine;
Human am I, the other is divine."

"No maid unmans the man can so make stand
'Gainst them that lord it in a new-born land":
So mused the tried old sire, and, musing so—
As once his Jove—he let the battle go.
The sire had notions. "Adolph and Ninette,
They be a parlous pair," he said. "Abet.
Oppose? Not I. No, not a single word
To Alcibiades or to the bird."

It was down by a spring that bubbled up
Among the hazels; with a glossy cup
Of leaves, Ninette was dipping, sipping, like
The smooth noon-bird she was. "Strike, sunlight, strike
Her head; and in your pretty beating say,
So does love punish, neither will it stay
More cruel stroke if straight you do not own
Your heart is Adolph's, his, and his alone."
So spoke the youth in thought, then, prying through
The maze of hazels, trolled he verses two
Of an old ditty,—

>   "*On a day it fell*
> *He found a naiad by her native well.*"
> She turned on him swift as the darting light
> Sunned water glances, putting out his sight
> With the flash of beauty,—"Thus he did begin:
> ' *Prithee, sweet love,*' and straight she pushed him in."

If, sire, your happy Hellas had its art
Supreme, what had this little darling heart
Here in the wild? The while love's arrow sped
Against her, up she tossed her glossy head
In golden scorn: "Play me a tune of war,
The iron string, the stave man's hands are for!
But Venus' viol!"

                         Stung by lesser thing,
The lordly creature seeks the herb will bring
Its life back: Adolph tasted, here and there,
All substances on which large love may fare,
Sore wounded. Now he nibbled at a book,
A good old tome that from its rusty nook
Looked out on him in pity; now he tried
The cures that grew the virgin brook beside,
Where strayed the bright-eyed scholar,
    breathless, pale,
His friend at last. All was of no avail;
Forthwith the maid, the lesser, frailer thing,
Was sure to turn anew and softly sting.
But, ah, the lonely upland roundelay
She sang in the clear space where all the day
The wild doves come! There with the gray
    wild dove,
It was another song, her song of love:—

"'Twixt the little oaks the sunbeams pry,
And, warm and gold, in the open lie;
    Yea, pretty doves,
    So many loves,
And to spare not one!
There be that have loves none.

"Around the doe plays the dappled fawn,
The rabbits dance at dusk and at dawn;
    Yea, pretty doves,
    So many loves,
And to spare not one!
There be that have loves none.

"The chatting squirrel, silver-gray,
Tells merry love-tales all the day;
    Yea, pretty doves,
    So many loves,
Every heart with its own;
And yet you moan, you moan."

THE little lonely upland song of love,
Crooned in the clear space with the
mourning-dove,
This nature heard, and, down below, the pain
Of the strong man; but came the two again
Together, not a sound she heard of all.
"The man would stir my love must fight, ay, fall,
For me; and though an angel came to say
'Sir Love does love thee,' I would turn away":
Thus mischievous Ninette. Her father gone,
Her uncle, too, and Cactus with him, on
A happy plan she hit, aided, may be,
By certain nettling words dropped craftily
By Hector's only master.

"Shall a man
Stand back for Hector! What my Shadow can,
It seems a man cannot. Set Hector food,
Prove Love for once could make his great words good."
"'T is well," the other answered; "cast or west,
Who challenges the Knight of Eagle Nest!
If Hector, joust with Hector let it be."

HE knight passed in to face armed Hector. He
Set food; Hector, responding with a thrust,
Caught him, sent him down headlong.
　　　　Mailed in dust,
Sir Love, no sooner down than up, would try
It out, now, humbled in his lady's eye.
'Twixt sport and earnest, evenly he strove
With rousing, pressing Hector till he drove
Three short, blunt prongs into his naked side.
Ninette, not seeing this, thinking he tried
To frighten her with show of danger, bade
Him yield the fight if, truly, use he had
For butcher's blade. But when she saw the tide
Slow reddening down the white of his bare side,
She flew to fetch the silver-hilted knife
Swung on the cabin wall. It was now life
Or death. Both little hands on, all her weight
To plunge the blade in, straight it went; so
　　　　straight,
Just back of Adolph's body as he held
Round Hector's neck, that prone the brute was
　　　　felled.
The knight fell with him.

Side by side they lay,
One dead, the other—'t was too soon to say.

The days were many ere she let him speak,
The boy she held from death, but when, still weak,
The words would come, then fell the voice of all
Voices the sweetest: "'He must fight, ay, fall,
For me.' In sorry truth, it has been done."
She smiling, weeping, answered, "Too well won."
Never before the wooing birds gave ear
So close; for never melody so dear
Was heard from mountain stream or mountain bough.
The naiad's heart was making music, now,
And happy Adolph answering,—"Death is gone,
Sweet; I remain; and here will I woo on
Till hale again; then hence, a knight well tried,
For home, my lance and lady at my side."

SO spoke the knightly heart, the knightly word
    Of cheer.   But one there was that overheard,
One all forgot in their full joy, his heart
Rankling with hatred, he whose hellish art
Had so miscarried.   On a fateful day
The two had wandered to the ledges gray,
Under the "flying bridge,"—the hanging pine,
With roots that push into midair, to twine
There, gnarled and naked.   Adolph thought to wind
His way out.   At the moment, close behind,
A footfall; and, as sprung up from the ground,
The fiend was on him.   Worn, weak with a wound—
Nay, 't is too horrible.   Let us hasten here,
As is the vintage children's wont, for fear
They in their dreams will see the cruel fight,
See Adolph, all but lost, summon his might,
And end it; see the reptile Cactus, hurled,
Writhing, into the hungry under-world.

To the far-off home was borne the mountain bride.

A WILD, rude tale; and true! At the fireside
Up in the hills, when summertime is gone,
And heavily the autumn rains come on,
The vintagers oft tell it, word for word,
Drinking huge bumpers to the "mountain-
    bird,"
Wishing her joy, she and her blue-eyed knight;
And full as heartily they cheer the flight
Of Cactus down the gulf, and curse his bones,
Left to the vultures. But among the stones
Under the pine, where all the summer day
The vintage children sport the time away,
Is oftener told the gentle afterpart
Of this grim Redwoods story; and the heart
Is in each little mouth as, one by one,
They wonder how the miracle
    was done.

A miracle it was: when next the flowers
Came out, upon a day of golden hours
There sprung, among the rocks around the pine,
The strangest, loveliest blossom that may shine
At any time, in any place. The earth
Has not another like it; for its birth
Was of the blood of her, the golden-haired,
Slight wounded by the weapon Cactus bared,
And she struck from him. Never tongue shall tell
How fair the flower the children love so well,
The rare rock-flower — one for each drop that fell —
They pluck, and call the Golden Lily-Bell.

FINIS